ADULT-ish

CRISTINA VANKO
(an adult)

A TARCHER PERIGEE ~~BOOK~~

tarcherperigee

An imprint of Penguin Random House LLC
375 Hudson Street
New York, New York 10014

Most TarcherPerigee books are available at special quantity discounts for bulk purchase for sales promotions, premiums, fund-raising, and educational needs. Special books or book excerpts also can be created to fit specific needs. For details, write: SpecialMarkets@ penguinrandomhouse.com.

ISBN 9780143129813

Printed in the United States of America
10 9 8 7 6 5 4 3 2 1

Book design by Cristina Vanko

TO THE PEOPLE WHO STOOD THE TEST OF TIME
AND ARE STILL INCLUDED IN MY PHONE BOOK.

AND THAT INCLUDES—
MY ARTSY DAD, MY NOT-SO-ARTSY MOM, MY SISTER, MARIA, AND
HER STYLISH CLOSET; MY NIECE, ADDY, MY BROTHER, TOMMY; AND SPUNKY.

MY MUNSTER HIGH SCHOOL GANG—
MY BESTIES DESIRÉE, KRISTY, KATIE, AND LAUREN, AND JOEL, MARA,
JEFF, AUSTIN, EUNICE, AND MY WONDERFUL TEACHER, MADAME MART-WEBB.

MY COLLEGE PALS (GO HOOSIERS!)—
LINDSAY, KATHERINE, DEREK, NATHANIEL, NIC, MISSY, LAURA, NICK, JESS, ESTHER,
ANNIE, CLAIRE, BRITTANY, STEPHANIE, ALYSHA, DANIELLE, AND MY BFA
CLASS THESIS CREW (THANKS FOR THE MIDNIGHT FRO-YO RUNS!).

MY INDIANAPOLIS FRIENDS—
MY PARTNERS-IN-CRIME, HALEY & NATALIE; JULIA, RITA, MAYOWA,
DENVER, MATT, DYLAN, GABE, ANTHONY, JULIE, AND DAN.

MY CHICAGO CREW—
MATT (AKA BAE), EILEEN, MISSY, AND ALL MY FRIENDS THAT DON'T
HAVE DIETARY RESTRICTIONS LIKE JESS, AMANDA G., AMANDA M.,
SAM, ESTEE, KRISTEN, LARA, JAMES, CHER, AND SUBI.

YOU ALL MADE ME THE ADULT I AM TODAY.

CERTIFICATE of BIRTH into ADULTHOOD

NAME _____

HEIGHT _____ WEIGHT _____

BIRTHDATE _____

PARENTS _____

PLACE OF BIRTH
INTO ADULTHOOD _____

adult

adjective | \ə-ˈdəlt, ˈa-ˌdəlt\

: fully grown and developed
: mature and sensible
: of or intended for adults

HOW OLD ARE YOU?
DRAW YOUR AGE.

are you an adult?

☐ YES
☐ NO
☐ MAYBE (please explain)

ON ADULTHOOD—

WHEN I WAS A LITTLE KID,
I THOUGHT THE MOMENT
YOU TURNED 16, YOU TURNED
INTO A *GROWN-UP.*
I MEAN, YOU COULD DRIVE.
YOU COULD GO <u>ANYWHERE</u>.
YOU WERE EVEN TALL ENOUGH
TO RIDE ALL THE ROLLERCOASTERS
AT AMUSEMENT PARKS. YOU
COULD WATCH MOVIES THAT
WEREN'T RATED PG AND YOU
COULD WATCH THEM ALL NIGHT
BECAUSE YOU DIDN'T HAVE A
BEDTIME. YOU WOKE UP IN THE
MORNING, DRANK A MAGIC POTION
THAT TASTES LIKE DIRT (A.K.A. COFFEE)
THAT KEEPS YOU AWAKE,
AND WENT TO THIS PLACE
CALLED "WORK." YOU WERE EVEN
ABLE TO EAT ICE CREAM FOR
BREAKFAST, IF YOU REALLY WANTED.
IT WAS PLAIN AND SIMPLE:
<u>YOU MADE THE RULES.</u>

WHEN YOU WERE YOUNGER,
WHAT QUALITIES DID YOU
THINK DEFINED WHAT IT
MEANT TO BE AN ADULT?

How to be an adult?

COMPLETING SCHOOL

LEAVING HOME

FINANCIAL INDEPENDENCE

STARTING A FAMILY

MARRIAGE

How many fifths of an adult are you?

What?! We're defining our life in pie slices now? That's both ridiculous and delicious. To some, these are the five conventions that define what it means to be a grown-up. To me, this is silly. There's so much more to life than these five things in defining our adult existence. In this book you will add many more itty-bitty slices to your recipe of adulthood, and that is just fine!

IT'S FUNNY HOW THINGS CHANGE ONCE
YOU ACTUALLY BECOME A GROWN-UP, RIGHT?
FIRST OFF, THERE ARE SO MANY CONFLICTING
DEFINITIONS. THE GOVERNMENT MAY SAY ONE
THING, YOUR BODY MAY SAY SOMETHING TOTALLY
DIFFERENT... ALL OF THIS IS JUST CONFUSING,
AS IF GROWING UP WEREN'T HARD ENOUGH.
WHILE YOU MAY NOT POSSESS ALL THE QUALITIES THAT
TRULY DEFINE WHAT IT MEANS TO BE AN ADULT,
THERE ARE CERTAIN MOMENTS THAT MAKE US FEEL
MORE LIKE WE'VE MASTERED ELEMENTS OF WHAT
IT MEANS TO BE A FULLY FUNCTIONING GROWN HUMAN.
THIS JOURNAL IS FOR CELEBRATING JUST THOSE
MOMENTS. IT'S FOR MARKING THE SMALL VICTORIES
TO OUR STEPS TO ADULTHOOD. IT'S ABOUT REMEMBERING
WHAT MATTERS MOST AS WE GROW OLDER AND
"MATURE" INTO THE BEST VERSION OF OUR
GROWN-UP SELVES.

THROUGHOUT THIS BOOK, DRAW, PAINT, WRITE,
COLLAGE—JUST DO WHATEVER FEELS RIGHT
FOR EACH PAGE. GO IN ORDER, OR SKIP AROUND,
THERE ISN'T A SET PATH.

Age ain't nothing but a number.

—AALIYAH

YOU'VE GOT THE LICENSE TO DRIVE. FILL IT IN.

DRIVER LICENSE

DRAW THE CAR YOU FIRST LEARNED TO DRIVE IN.

WHO DID YOU FREAK OUT, I MEAN,
WHO DID YOU TAKE ALONG FOR THE RIDE?

WHERE'D YOU LEARN?

WHAT HAPPENED?

CAN YOU STILL PARALLEL PARK?
yes ☐ no ☐

a tribute to

What's the first household
appliance that you really wanted? This page is
a tribute to that amazing, life-changing
object of your desire.

Close your eyes. You just graduated. You're a blank canvas. Paint a picture of your first thoughts entering the real world.

USE A PENCIL TO MAP OUT WHERE YOUR FRIENDS ARE. IT'S LIKELY THAT YOUR PALS WILL RELOCATE MULTIPLE TIMES, SO UPDATE ACCORDINGLY!

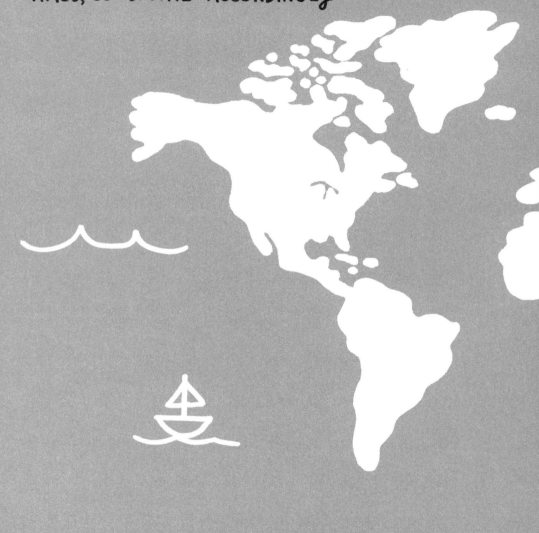

MAKE SURE YOU HAVE A ~~GOOD~~ ERASER. THE AVERAGE
AMERICAN MOVES 11.7 TIMES IN THEIR LIFESPAN!

You're renting your first apartment. Here's a handy list of things to look (and wish!) for:

- ☐ HAS MORE THAN ONE ROOM... OR AT LEAST ROOM FOR EVERYTHING I NEED.
- ☐ BEDROOM FITS MORE THAN A BED?
- ☐ BONUS POINTS FOR A CLOSET.
- ☐ QUIET ENOUGH TO SLEEP AT NIGHT?
- ☐ GETS ENOUGH NATURAL LIGHT TO KEEP THE PLANTS ALIVE.
- ☐ ASSURANCE THAT YOUR CLOTHES WON'T GO TOO LONG WITHOUT BEING WASHED...
- ☐ A DISHWASHER!
- ☐ HAS ENOUGH OUTLETS TO KEEP YOU PLUGGED IN
- ☐ SHOWER IS IN THE BATHROOM
- ☐ NEIGHBORHOOD
- ☐ IS THERE COFFEE? ☐ PIZZA? ☐ A BAR? IMPORTANT CONSIDERATIONS.
- ☐ DECENT DISTANCE FROM PUBLIC TRANSIT? ☐ WORK? ☐ GROCERY ☐ PARK? ☐ GYM?
- ☐ GOOD FRIENDS NEARBY? OR MAYBE IN THE SAME APARTMENT!
- ☐ PARKING SITUATION FOR CARS? ☐ BIKES?

Remember to bring a check and measuring tape with you!

No worries if you had to boomerang back to mama and papa bear for a bit after graduation. What matters is that you did it—you flew away from the nest!
Now, show off your first place!

If you haven't ventured away just yet, what do you think your apartment will look like?

WHAT'S THE SITCH WITH THE LIVING SITUATION?
WHO WAS (WERE) YOUR FIRST ROOMMATE(S)?

My AWESOME ROOMIE

NAME(S):

BIRTHDAY(S):

OCCUPATION(S):

HOW YOU MET:

FAVORITE ACTIVITY YOU ENJOY DOING TOGETHER:

FAVORITE SNACK(S):

Roommate
HALL of FAME

Where did you spend the first night partying in your new 'hood?

PARTY ON!

 **Cheers!** DESIGN THE COASTER THAT COMMEMORATES YOUR FIRST LEGAL DRINK.

DID YOU SIP IT AT THE STROKE OF MIDNIGHT?

WHAT'S YOUR FAVORITE FANCY COCKTAIL NOW?

WHERE WAS IT? WHO WAS WITH YOU?

Long gone are the days of putty-ing up posters in your dorm room. What are you framing in your adultified apartment?

These works of art may be worth millions one day!

DIY projects can turn out to be a braggable success or an utter disaster. How did your first home project stack up?

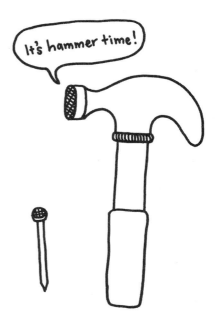

WHAT'S IN YOUR FRIDGE RIGHT NOW?

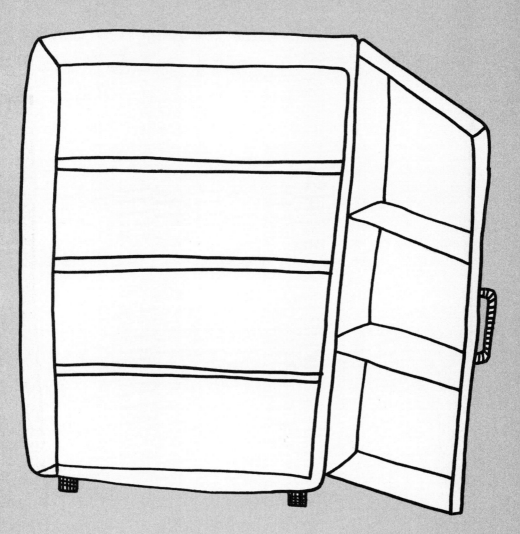

I know, I know. It's hard enough feeding yourself and looking somewhat presentable on a daily basis. Draw a picture of the first houseplant you kept alive.

Finally. You're responsible and ready.
Adopt that cute, cuddly animal you've
been dying to have. Post a picture here.

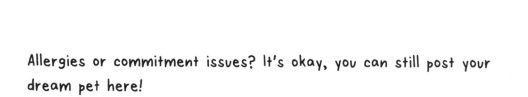

Allergies or commitment issues? It's okay, you can still post your
dream pet here!

This page may unintentionally show your age since we're talking technology here. Draw your first cellular device.

If it's kinda boxy, you guessed it, you're a bit on the older side ;)

What kept you awake the first time you stayed up all night just talking about life?

WHAT WAS YOUR FIRST "I'M REALLY STRESSED BECAUSE I NEED TO GET _____ DONE" ALL-NIGHTER?

your 1st BIG interview!

you ROCKED IT!
HOW DID you DO IT?

WOMP. WOMP.
HOW DID you BOMB
LIKE THAT?

JOB INTERVIEW TALLY BOX

I'M A(N) _____ at _____.
I'M SO EXCITED TO...

YOU'RE TOO LEGIT TO QUIT.
WHAT DOES YOUR FIRST BUSINESS CARD LOOK LIKE?

YOUR FIRST DAY ON THE JOB!
HOW'D IT GO?

Did you find the bathroom ok?

Are there free snacks?

DRAW YOUR OUTFIT.

It's your first payday and you're rolling in the dough! What did you purchase with your first real-job paycheck? Draw it here.

PAY DAY!

pay to: _____ $ [   ]

_____

memo: J-O-B _____

First cup of coffee you enjoyed...

...just to function in the morning

...for networking purposes

...as a major bonding experience

...reuniting with an old friend

...wait, was that just a date?

...that was definitely a date!

What are you saving for?
It could be as boring as renting
an apartment with built-in laundry
or as extraordinary
as a beach vacation.

BANK

*REMEMBER TO SAVE SOME MONEY
  FOR LATE ADULTHOOD TOO!

CROSS OUT ITEMS WHEN YOU ACCOMPLISH A SAVINGS GOAL.

of DREAMS

Come to think of it, an apartment with built-in laundry is quite luxurious.

BUT all the!
magic
I HAVE
KNOWN
I'VE HAD TO
MAKE MYSELF

-Shel Silverstein

Matchmaking is an art, not a science. Have you been a successful matcher or matchee? What's your secret?

People I'd like to find a mate for:

KEEP TRACK OF ALL THE TIMES YOU'VE SAID "I'M NEVER DRINKING AGAIN" HERE.

SECRETS ARE NO FUN.

What's your hangover remedy?

SHARE IT WITH AN UP-AND-COMING ADULT.

Many of us find that our parents become our friends. Here's to our oldest friends — the ones we've been with since before we were born.

Dad's corniest joke:

Best parental advice received so far:

Mom's favorite piece of jewelry:

Who are the smartest, funniest, trustworthiest, or otherwise most awesome relatives? What makes them such MVPs in your adult life?

RECORD ALL YOUR PAST BROKEN RELATIONSHIPS AND FLINGS HERE.

Now, cross those names out. Scribble them out of your life for good! Didn't that feel good? The first time you delete them on your phone feels even more phenomenal. You should do that too. (Right about now!)

WHAT'S THE FIRST SONG THAT MADE YOU FEEL OUT OF TOUCH WITH KIDS TODAY?

_____ BY: _____

OK, ENOUGH OF THAT. LET'S MAKE A PLAYLIST. POST YOUR GREATEST HITS THAT MAKE YOU SHAKE WHAT YOUR MAMA GAVE YOU. WHO CARES IF THEY'RE NOT "HIP"!

1.

2.

3.

4.

5.

6.

7.

8.

9.

10.

FEELING COMFORTABLE IN YOUR OWN SKIN IS A BIG PART OF ADULTHOOD. WHAT WAS YOUR BREAKTHROUGH FEEL-GOOD MOMENT?

COOKING FRIENDSGIVING AWAY FROM HOME

$ GETTING MY FIRST RAISE

GOING ON MY FIRST VACATION

Write a letter to the first friend that comes to mind. Yes, let's get old school. Use a pen and paper! Tell them all the reasons you appreciate them. Sign, seal, and deliver it (through the mail).

hi!

Make sure you acquire stamps before sending it. This ain't email!

Draw the first bouquet of flowers you've ever received or sent to someone special.

Little things like this aren't cheesy.
They're wonderful. You're quite the darling.

What makes you you down to the core? What traits will you always carry with you everywhere you go, no matter how young or old you are? Use this space as your identity toolbox.

you

For me, I would include my love for dessert. Share what you're about with #AdultishBook!

WHAT WAS YOUR FIRST "ADULT MOVE"?

FOR ME, IT'S NOT HAVING MY DIRTY LAUNDRY ACCOMPANY ME WHEN I VISIT MY PARENTS' HOUSE.

TREAT yourself

Go on a date with yourself. Yes, you heard that right.
Treat yourself. Appreciate the freedom and time spent alone.
Reflect on good experiences and relax, you awesome adult, you!

First date pro-tip:
Don't check your phone.

TOO SMALL OF A SPACE? WELL, LET'S MOVE ON!
WHAT DID YOU LEARN FROM THE EXPERIENCE?

It turns out you can teach an old dog new tricks. What's something valuable that you've learned as an adult?

Social media can be silly enough to make you LOL for real.
But sometimes it can make us feel like grown-ups too.
List some of those moments here.

HA!

LOLZ

hehe

ROFL

lmao

HAHA

lawwrwl

If selfies weren't bad enough, when did we go from that to
talking how bad traffic is? Yeesh!

HOW DO YOU ROLL?
DRAW YOUR FIRST
SET OF GROWN-UP WHEELS.

Does this sweet ride have a name? Write it down here:

WHEN YOU'RE NOT "MAKING IT," IT'S EASY TO GET JEALOUS OF A FRIEND'S SUCCESS. BUT AS WE AGE, THAT JEALOUSY TURNS INTO HAPPINESS, BECAUSE WE COME TO UNDERSTAND THAT THERE'S NO COMPETITION WITH ANYONE EXCEPT OURSELVES. TELL ME HOW YOUR FRIENDS ARE KILLING IT!

Who was your first friend to get married? They're like real adults now...they could even start a family soon, with mini versions of themselves, ahem, I mean babies! Thoughts? Feelings? A good story? SPILL.

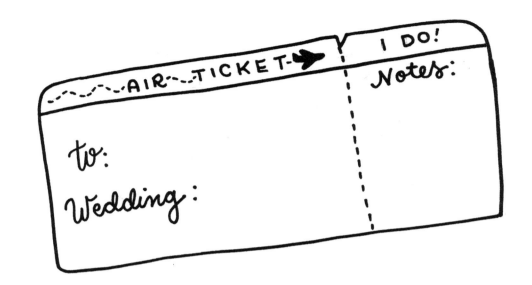

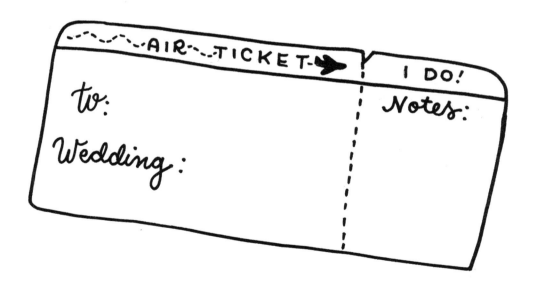

You're going to go on so many vacations...I mean, use up your vacation time for friends' weddings.

WHETHER YOU ULTIMATELY SWIPED LEFT (OR RIGHT!) IRL, DISH THE DEETS FROM YOUR FIRST ONLINE DATING EXPERIENCE.

There's a certain point in life that our social media timelines become engulfed with sparkly rings and serious relationships. Whenever a friend gets engaged, draw the ring here.

ROADTRIPS ARE ALWAYS BETTER WITH A FRIEND.
WHERE ON THE OPEN ROAD DID you CRUISE OFF TO?

WHAT DID you SEE?

ANYTHING INTERESTING ON
THE SIDE OF THE ROAD?

HOW MANY MILES
DID you TRAVEL?

Letting someone or something very dear to you go is a part of growing up. How did this shape who you are?

WRITE *your* ADULT MANTRA REALLY BIG

*USE PENCIL. THIS COULD CHANGE.

Commitment, spiders, and bills, oh my!
Describe the first time you did something
you were really afraid of.

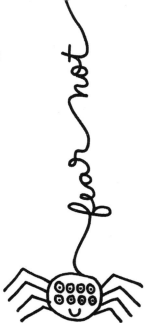

PAGE OF REGRETS

TEXTING THAT PERSON YOU SHOULDN'T HAVE.

SLEEPING IN UNTIL 3 P.M.

EATING THAT WHOLE PIZZA BY MYSELF...
OKAY THIS ACTUALLY DESERVES A RIBBON!

Solo travel is an empowering part of becoming an adult, and should be a requirement! What did you learn about yourself on that first trip?

No more emotional baggage!

Use #AdultishBook to share some of those memories.

What was your first big move? Was it a new city? A new job? A new love interest?

If you've never complimented a complete stranger before, get out there and make that your mission. Draw the first lovely compliment you gave below.

Love your smile!

You don't have to wait until mid-life to have an existential crisis. Now they come even sooner! Don't sweat it. It's normal. Describe the first time you felt lost.

How did you find yourself again?

sew Cool

Don't wait until you're a grandparent. Book clubs, knitting, and pottery class are actually are a lot cooler than you might think. What was the first hobby you took up as an adult?

From running 26.2 miles to marathoning your favorite TV show, what's the first thing you've done that you once thought was impossible?

IT'S NORMAL TO MISS SCHOOL SOMETIMES ONCE YOU GRADUATE TO THE "REAL WORLD." DESCRIBE THE FIRST TIME YOU MISSED ACADEMIA.

Big speeches and presentations can be terrifying. How did you feel when it was over?

Uncertainty is so,
so underrated.

—JOHN GREEN

Whether you're engaged to a human or a
slice of pizza, draw a silly engagement photo.

SO IN LOVE

 *mwah!*

Don't keep your lips sealed!
Who was your best kiss?

Who was your most recent kiss?

WHEN WAS THE FIRST TIME YOU SPOKE UP
FOR SOMETHING YOU REALLY BELIEVE IN?

HOW ABOUT THE FIRST TIME YOU
FELT VULNERABLE?

What's the first recipe that you really mastered?

Recipe

Who did you share the deliciousness with?

What only exists on the weekends, and can be boozier than New Year's Eve? Brunch!
Describe the first time you brunched like a boss.

Tell us about the tastiness with #AdultishBook.

DO YOU DANCE AROUND IN AN OVERSIZED BUTTON-DOWN, UNDIES, AND SOCKS? OR LEAP FOR JOY? WHAT'S YOUR REACTION WHEN PLANS ARE CANCELLED?

CHOOSE ONE

🏠 RENT **or** HAPPY HOUR 🍷

We all know it's much easier to give advice to others than follow it ourselves. What was the first really good bit of guidance you gave yourself?

Bright idea.

Move over, hand-me-downs. Draw the first piece of furniture you purchased for yourself.

BRAND NEW!

Adults visit museums a little differently from everyone else.
Ever read all the information cards in an exhibit room?
Give it a try – and then record what you learned.

Really Cool Thing
2016

You will learn neat
facts by reading this.
Everyone will be
very impressed.

What's the first trendy word or phrase you had to look up, now that you're a sophisticated adult? What does it mean?

TO INK OR NOT TO INK, THAT IS THE QUESTION.
WHETHER OR NOT YOU'VE TAKEN THE PLUNGE,
WHAT'S YOUR FIRST TATTOO?

Let's hear about those sorta cute babies you've met so far.

Is it just me, or do babies look like aliens sometimes?

Whether it's a baby human or even a baby puppy, kitty, or pet iguana, list some future baby names here.

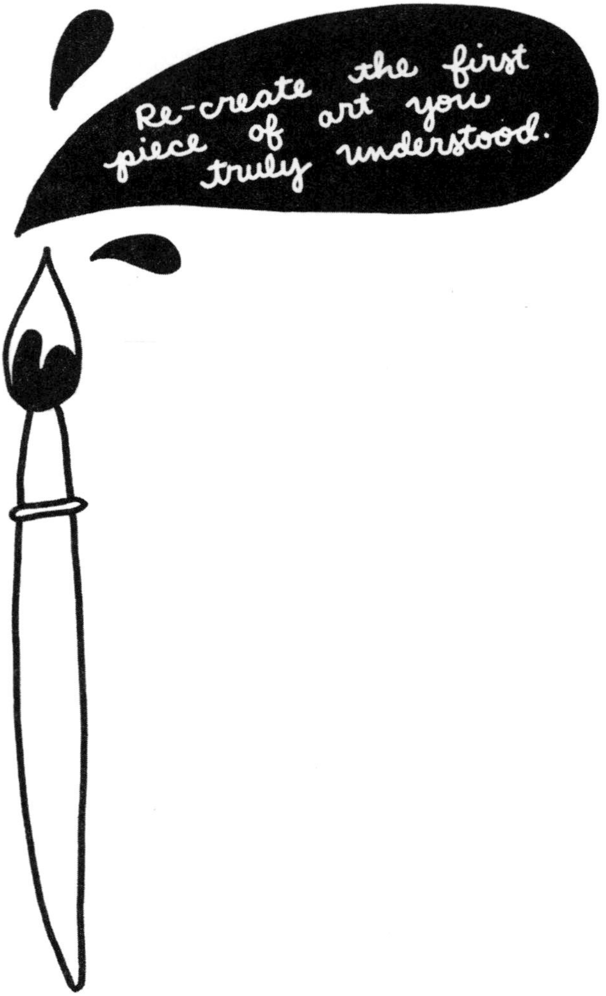

I'm like SO impressed.

LIFE IS A MIXTAPE. WHAT ARE SOME SONGS THAT CARRY MEANING TO YOU WHENEVER YOU HEAR THEM?

my first time...

WORK PLAYLIST:

WHAT ARE THE TUNES THAT GET YOU
IN THE WORKDAY GROOVE?

THIS ONE DESERVES A TROPHY.
WHAT'S THE FIRST BIG GOAL THAT YOU
REACHED AS A FOCUSED AND DRIVEN ADULT?

WHAT ARE YOUR OTHER GOALS? LIST THEM BELOW, AND GRAPH WHERE YOU'RE AT IN YOUR QUEST TO REACH THEM.

PROGRESS

GOALS

Did you dress up? Did you order food that you couldn't quite pronounce? Spill the deets about your very first fancy date.

Gush here about the first time you had thoughts about marrying that dreamy significant other of yours (or maybe you've already tied the knot).

I hope that special someone still makes your heart go pitter-patter!

WHAT'S ON YOUR BUCKET LIST?

CREATE A FRIENDSHIP BRACELET FOR THE FIRST CLOSE FRIEND YOU MADE ON THE INTERNET.

What was the first job you got in the industry you've always wanted to be in?

If you're one of those rare gems who started out in your preferred industry, what was your first big accomplishment there?

Write all
the advice
from your
first mentor.
→never forget it.

The sky's the limit!

Have you ever showed up to the airport with bags and no place to go? Yes?! No? Either way, let's hear about your first spontaneous adventure.

Still separating your Oreos before you eat them? Picking all the chocolate chips out of the trail mix? Leaving your sandwich crusts uneaten? What childhood food habits are you still hanging on to?

Any grown-up culinary milestones to celebrate?

This page is your makeshift passport! Stamp it with all the countries you've visited as an adult.

Relaxation Playlist

1.

2.

3.

4.

5.

6.

7.

8.

9.

10.

YOU KNOW YOU'RE AN ADULT WHEN...

Looking forward to buying your own home someday?
Sketch your dream home here.

Picket fence or nah?

Breakups stink, end of story. Recount your first grown-up heartbreak here.

SOME AMAZING HUMANS OUT THERE TOO!

More important are the butterfly feelings. Let those feelings guide your words as you describe the first time you fell in love as a full-fledged (ish) adult.

Now that you're a grown-up, it's your turn to treat a younger relative or friend to a nice dinner, show, or night on the town. Describe how you paid it forward here:

WORDS TO LIVE BY

Even as adults, we need the wisdom of others. Gather some grown-up advice from the following:

a family member:

an old friend:

a coworker:

a neighbor:

a doctor:

a business leader:

a child:

a dog owner:

a lawyer:

an artist:

Being able to empathize with others for the first time is life-changing. Take a walk in someone else's shoes. How'd your perspective shift?

Enjoy going through life as yourself

—LENA DUNHAM

The first time you volunteer for a cause you really believe in does you and the community good.

DESCRIBE ALL THE FEEL-GOOD MOMENTS.

what's the first song you actually paid for?

THE *first* TIME YOU SAID "NO" AND REALLY MEANT IT

the FIRST TIME YOU SAID "Yes" AND REALLY MEANT IT

When you're living in different places, your friends and family are all leading different lives. Hard to imagine, right? How'd your first visit to a far-away loved one go?

WE ALL MESS UP SOMETIMES.
DESCRIBE YOUR FIRST BIG "OOPS" AS AN ADULT.
WRITE IT DOWN AND LET IT GO.

LOOK BACK ON YOUR SOCIAL MEDIA TIMELINES, AND
COLLAGE YOUR VERY FIRST POSTS HERE. HOW HAS
YOUR ONLINE PERSONA CHANGED SINCE THEN?

First wrinkle: _____

First gray hair: _____

First backache: _____

≥ I'M CUTTING THIS LIST OFF! ≤

THESE THINGS HAPPEN, AND YOU SHOULDN'T DWELL ON IT TOO MUCH. AGING HAPPENS!

POST A PICTURE OF YOURSELF.

 12889 likes

Adult-ish Whatta babe!

Lessons are learned long after we graduate. What was the first meaningful life lesson you learned as an adult?

Write "hangovers are no fun" until your hangover goes away.

WATCHING YOUR FIRST SPORTS GAME IN REAL LIFE IS SO MUCH MORE FUN THAN WATCHING IT ON TELEVISION. THERE ARE STADIUM SNACKS AND SUPERFANS — WHAT'S NOT TO LOVE? AS A GROWN-UP, WHAT WAS YOUR FIRST PROFESSIONAL GAME?

HOW ABOUT YOUR FIRST CONCERT AS AN ADULT?
DID YOU SHAKE WHAT YOUR MAMA GAVE YOU?

RATE THE PERFORMANCE:

☆ ☆ ☆ ☆ ☆

WHAT DO you VALUE MOST AS AN ADULT?
LIST SOME THINGS you HOLD CLOSE TO YOUR HEART.

Friends I can count on

When the barista knows
my order by heart

Sleeping in on the weekend

Feeling the spring sunshine on
my face after a long winter

Always stick up for how awesome you are.
When was the first time you proved yourself?

You rule.

Time seems to pass so slowly when you're young, and then it flies by when you're an adult. But this makes sense. When you're two years old, 1 year = half of your life. Then, when you're 20 years, old 1 year = 5% of your life. When did you first notice time fly?

ANOTHER WAY PEOPLE MEASURE TIME IS IN
MEMORABLE EVENTS. WHAT ARE SOME OF THOSE
DEFINING MOMENTS AT EACH AGE? FILL THEM
IN BELOW.

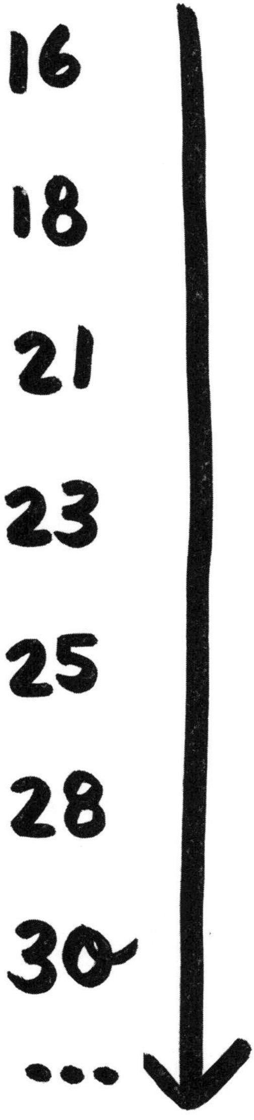

16

18

21

23

25

28

30

...

Even if it was just trading a snack with someone at work, what was your first big negotiation?

What's your go-to beverage order?

Bonus points for drawing pretty pictures in the foam!

Finally growing out that mohawk, or trimming those super-long locks? Document your first look-altering haircut. Post or draw before and after pics below.

So fresh!

Difficult conversations can be daunting. But once you have that talk, it's like a huge weight has been lifted off your shoulders. What was your first tough conversation?

GHOSTING IS THE WORST. WHEN DID YOU DECIDE TO BREAK UP LIKE A CIVILIZED HUMAN BEING?

THIS IS THE PAGE WHERE YOU COMPLAIN ABOUT BILLS, INSURANCE, AND THE THINGS YOU WISH YOU DIDN'T HAVE TO SPEND YOUR HARD-EARNED CASH ON.

Tell me about the first big risk you've taken.

Whenever I go to art museums, I may or may not break out some art history lingo I learned in school. I toss out terms like contrapposto, chiaroscuro, and sprezzatura. Boom! What was your first nerdy moment of glory?

NO MATTER HOW MATURE OR IMMATURE THESE
RESPONSES MAY BE, WRITE DOWN SOME OF
YOUR FAVORITE ADULT THINGS HERE.

favorite book:

favorite food:

favorite holiday:

favorite sport:

favorite movie:

favorite celebrity:

favorite music:

favorite hangout spot:

favorite season:

favorite coffee shop:

favorite friend(s):

favorite city:

favorite hobby:

Taste buds change every seven years, so it's safe to assume your palate has matured. What are some foods that you like now that you may not have fancied when you were younger? Record a newfound recipe here.

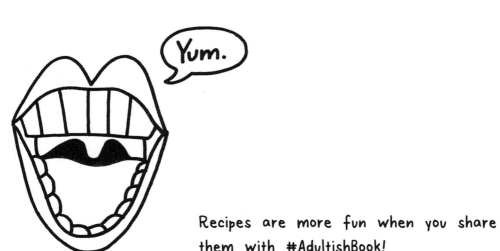

Yum.

Recipes are more fun when you share them with #AdultishBook!

NOT ALL "BABIES" ARE HUMAN.
WHAT PROJECT, ACCOMPLISHMENT, OR OTHER
SHINING GLORY ARE YOU PROUDEST OF?
DO YOU HAVE ITS PHOTO IN YOUR WALLET,
OR A TATTOO OF ITS NAME ON YOUR...?

Comfort > Cute...most of the time. Draw the first practical item of clothing you purchased that you now can't imagine your life without.

Best choice ever

VACATION-ALL I EVER WANTED! WHERE DID YOU KICK BACK ON YOUR FIRST SELF-FUNDED TRIP?

_____ AND _____ SITTING ON A PLANE, K-I-S-S-I-N-G... SO WHERE WAS YOUR FIRST ROMANTIC GETAWAY?

The time has come for your first high school reunion. What was your first impression?

CLASS OF '

If you've got it,
FLAUNT IT.
And if you don't got it?
FLAUNT IT.
'Cause what are we even doing here if we're not flaunting it?

—MINDY KALING

Action!

CREATE A MOVIE POSTER
FOR YOUR LIFE STORY
(SO FAR).

WHICH CELEBRITY WILL PLAY THE STARRING ROLE?

Presidents have a holiday. Moms and dads do too.
What holiday would you like to create, to commemorate
a milestone or achievement you'll never forget?

REMEMBERED MY ROOMMATE'S BIRTHDAY

THE LOUD NEIGHBORS FINALLY MOVED OUT DAY

INDEPENDENCE DAY FROM THE ANNOYING EX

GOT A RAISE DAY

OFFICIALLY IN A RELATIONSHIP DAY

DO YOU HATE YOUR BIRTHDAY?
☐ YES ☐ NO

IF YES, PLEASE EXPLAIN. IF NO, COME BACK TO THIS QUESTION IN A FEW YEARS.

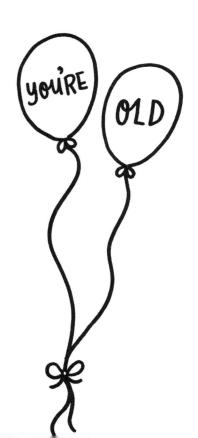

Wrapped with love (and a bow), what was the first gift you put some extra thought into for a someone special?

NOT MAKING IT HOME FOR THANKSGIVING CAN
BE A BUMMER. ON THE BRIGHT SIDE, NOW YOU'RE
ABLE TO MAKE IT ANYTHING YOU WANT IT TO BE
HOW DID YOU SPEND YOUR FIRST FRIENDSGIVING?

Did you order takeout?

Did you see a movie?

Did you spend it with friends?

IF YOU COULD CHOOSE YOUR FAMILY, WHO WOULD YOU INCLUDE?

The friend who tells you what not to wear ⊘

Your bestie

The fluffy dog that happens to live next door

NAME THE FIRST FRIEND THAT POPS INTO YOUR HEAD FOR THE FOLLOWING:

The Adventurer:

The Creative One:

The Advice Giver:

The One with a Cute Dog:

The Tastemaker:

The Foodie:

The Goal Pusher:

The Fun Haver:

The Health Nut:

The One You Could Always Count On:

The One with a Boat:

The Strong One:

The Smart One:

The One with a Good Sense of Humor:

HANG ON TO YOUR SQUAD FOREVER. REMEMBER TO CHECK IN WITH YOUR PALS EVERY ONCE IN A WHILE TO SEE HOW THEY'RE DOING. WHATEVER YOU DO, DON'T LET ADULTHOOD TAKE YOUR RELATIONSHIPS AWAY FROM YOU.

CREATE A SUPERHERO THAT CAPTURES THE GROWN-UP YOU MOST WANT TO BE. DON'T FORGET TO LIST YOUR SUPERPOWERS!

WRITE OUT A FAKE POLICE REPORT FOR THE FIRST ILLEGAL THING YOU EVER DID.

Did you know it's forbidden to eat watermelon in the park in the state of Indiana?

WHICH FICTIONAL CHARACTER BEST CHRONICLES YOUR GROWN-UP EXISTENCE?

THE BEST
THING ABOUT
BEING AN ADULT
SO FAR IS...

THE WORST THING ABOUT BEING AN ADULT SO FAR IS...

MY GROWN-UP GO-TOS

WEBSITE FOR GIGGLES:

COFFEE SHOP:

PARK FOR PEOPLE WATCHING:

CLOTHING STORE:

BOOKSTORE:

DATE SPOT:

FANCY RESTAURANT:

FAST-FOOD JOINT:

BASIC BAR:

DIVE BAR:

FANCY DRINK:

BEACH:

Red carpet or not, what's the most glamorous event you've attended?

ON A SCALE OF 1 to 10, HOW DID YOUR FIRST INTRODUCTION BETWEEN YOUR MAIN SQUEEZE AND YOUR PARENTS GO?

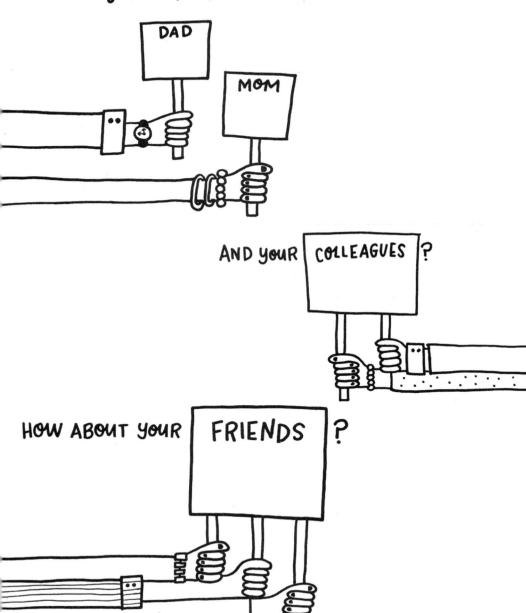

WHAT ARE YOUR WEIRDEST FIRSTS? ANY GOOD STORIES COME FROM THOSE EXPERIENCES?

Seeing your first shooting star and having the wish come true.

Being late to work and blaming ————.

Showing up at the wrong party

Running into that person you went on one date with   AWKS

Wearing your shirt inside out

A FRIEND ONCE TOLD ME "YOU CAN'T GO 60% SKYDIVING." IT'S ALL OR NOTHING. THAT PARTICULAR FRIEND HAS SHIFTED MY PERSPECTIVE ON A LOT OF THINGS IN LIFE. DESCRIBE A FRIEND WHO'S CHANGED YOUR LIFE FOREVER.

Things don't always turn out the way we planned. And that's not always a bad thing! What are the biggest surprises about adulthood so far?

So, what are we ordering tonight?

It turns out, I love bingeing on Chinese food and Netflix by myself!

We're all turning into our parents. Describe the moments when you most see this in action.

Is it just me, or do your parents love you even more when you visit them for the first time after you moved far away? What happened when you came back home for the first time?

If only all visits involved having your favorite pizza waiting for you.

Built it yourself? Commemorate the first piece of furniture that literally came in pieces here.

```
┌─────────────────────────────────────────┐
│  ⊘   COMMEMORATIVE PLAQUE        ⊘  │
└─────────────────────────────────────────┘
```

CONVERSE WITH YOUR 'RENTS

Q: "WHEN DID YOU FIRST RECOGNIZE THAT I TURNED INTO AN ADULT?"

A:

Q: "AS A FULLY FUNCTIONING HUMAN, WHEN DID I FIRST MAKE YOU PROUD?"

A:

Q: "WHERE WERE YOU IN LIFE AT MY AGE?"

A:

FROM YOUR HIGH SCHOOL EX'S HOUSE TO THAT DIVE BAR DOWN THE STREET, WHEN WAS THE FIRST TIME YOU THOUGHT, "I CAN'T BELIEVE I'M BACK HERE!" AS AN ADULT?

ADULTHOOD 101

It's only when you're out in the real world that you realize that school didn't teach you anything practical about life. Create a lesson plan of the things you'd like to teach kids who are about to graduate.

_____

_____

_____

_____

_____

_____

_____

_____

_____

_____

_____

_____

_____

_____

_____

_____

DESCRIBE THE FIRST TIME you COULD
LOOK BACK AND LAUGH ABOUT
_____ HAPPENING.

LIST YOUR FAVORITE NEW TRADITIONS HERE.

Tuesdays are my fave.

NOWADAYS, THERE'RE APP IDEAS FOR EVERYTHING UNDER THE SUN. WHAT'S YOUR FIRST BRILLIANT BUSINESS IDEA? MAKE IT HAPPEN!

I remember
the first time...

FLYING SOLO CAN BE KINDA NERVE-WRACKING.
WHEN DID YOU WEAR YOUR BIG-PERSON PANTS
AND FINALLY...

SHOP FOR NEW JEANS WITHOUT A SECOND OPINION

EAT DINNER AT A RESTAURANT SOLO

FLY ACROSS THE COUNTRY BY YOURSELF

HEAD OUT TO A PARTY WITHOUT A WINGMAN
(OR WINGWOMAN)

Spread your wings!

SEE A MOVIE ALONE

Hip-hip, hooray!

COMMEMORATE THE FIRST BIG LOAN YOU PAID OFF.

ONLY $ _____ TO GO!

IT TAKES A WISE GROWN-UP TO SAY,
"HOW IMMATURE I WAS!" LOOK AT YOU
NOW. WHEN WAS THE FIRST TIME YOU
SAID THIS?

My most awkward roommate moment was when I woke up one morning and discovered that my roommate had packed up everything and moved to another country without telling me. What's your weirdest roomie experience to date?

Okay, she did leave something behind. But it was an ungodly amount of eggs in the fridge... weird.

IT'S TRUE, WE ONLY LIVE ONCE. (EVEN OUR CATS!)
WHEN WAS THE FIRST TIME YOU TRULY
SEIZED THE DAY?

#YOLO

STICKY SITUATIONS AREN'T ONLY FOR HALLOWEEN. WHAT'S THE WORST STICKY SITUATION YOU'VE GOTTEN YOURSELF INTO? HOW DID YOU GET UNSTUCK?

DRAW your ADULT SPIRIT ANIMAL HERE.

It takes 21 days to form a habit, and 66 for it to stick... and if they're bad habits? Well, those take a whole lot of willpower to drop. What's the first bad habit you've kicked as an adult? What's next on your list?

WHAT'S YOUR FAVORITE PARTY?
NOOOO, NOT THAT TYPE OF PARTY. WE'RE TALKING
POLITICS. WHAT WAS THE FIRST ELECTION
YOU VOTED IN?

ELECTION YEAR_____

VOICE YOUR OPINIONS HERE. WE'RE LISTENING.

Sometimes after a long, exhausting week, there's nothing better than a mellow evening at home. What's your go-to plan for a Friday night in?

Practicing mixology? Finishing Lord of the Rings? Catching up on the cats of Instagram? Let's hear about it with #AdultishBook.

LIST ALL THE THINGS YOU LONG FOR FROM BACK IN THE DAY.

Nostalgia Page

SCENTED PENS. SLAP BRACELETS. SCRUNCHIES. OH! THOSE WERE THE DAYS!

Meeting your significant other's family is an adult rite of passage. How'd it go? What surprised you the most? And what helped you get the bigger picture?

WHEN I GET OLDER I WANT TO...

GIVE YOURSELF SOME CREDIT.
CREATE STICKERS FOR THE RESPONSIBLE,
ADULT-LIKE TASKS YOU'VE TACKLED
THIS WEEK.

CALLED the FAM!

DID MY LAUNDRY
BEFORE RUNNING
OUT OF CLEAN
✦ UNDERWEAR ✦

MY PAGE of ADULT-ACQUIRED TASTES

BLACK COFFEE

taking photos of sunsets

ENJOYING SOME DOWN TIME

DECLINING ONE-NIGHT STANDS

Avoiding gassy foods

BUYING THINGS

WEARING SENSIBLE SHOES ON SALE

eating stinky cheese GIVING UP your VICES

WATCHING YOUR WEIGHT GOING TO BED EARLY

IT'S MUCH EASIER
TO NOT KNOW
THINGS SOMETIMES.
THINGS CHANGE
AND FRIENDS LEAVE.
AND LIFE DOESN'T STOP
FOR ANYBODY.

—STEPHEN CHBOSKY

AT SOME POINT YOU'RE GOING TO REALIZE THAT
YOU HAVE A JOB AND A SOMEWHAT FULFILLING
LIFE WITH NEAT FRIENDS IN A COOL LOCATION.
THAT MEANS YOU'VE BASICALLY MADE IT, RIGHT?
THROW YOURSELF A "*Living the Dream*" PARTY.
DOCUMENT IT HERE.

What adult-like qualities do you have

Remember that absurd adult pie from the beginning? Well, here's a DIY pie this time. It could be a pizza pie, a chicken pot pie, a chocolate cream pie a la mode...the pie options are endless. Fill the pie in with all slices of life that make up adulthood for you.

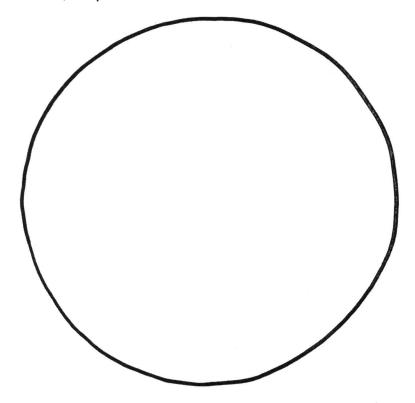

You're just a slice of heaven, aren't you?

IT'S THE END OF A BOOK. FOR SOME, THAT'S AN
ADULT-LIKE ACHIEVEMENT IN ITSELF! I'M GLAD YOU
MADE IT HERE. REMEMBER, BEING A GROWN-UP ISN'T
THE END OF YOUR LIFE. YEAH, YOU MAY BE AGING
AND "GROWING OLD," BUT THAT JUST MEANS THAT
YOU'RE GAINING MORE EXPERIENCE, LEARNING NEW
THINGS, AND FIGURING OUT WHO YOU REALLY ARE.
YOU DON'T NEED TO CHECK OFF ANY PRE-CONSTRUCTED
MILESTONES TO PROVE YOU'RE ""5/5THS ADULT"
AND YOU NEVER, EVER, EVER HAVE TO LOSE YOUR
CHILDLIKE SENSE OF JOY AND WONDER —
THAT'S TRULY WHAT KEEPS LIFE INTERESTING.

I'VE HEARD THE QUOTE ""DON'T GROW UP, IT'S A TRAP,"
BUT I'D LIKE TO THINK OF THIS HERE "TRAP" AS A
PUZZLE OF SORTS. WE'RE ALL JUST TRYING TO FIGURE
IT OUT, AND IF YOU STAY TRUE TO YOURSELF, YOU'LL
MAKE IT WORK IN YOUR OWN WAY. SO GO AHEAD,
MAKE MORE MEMORIES, DON'T DWELL, MOVE FORWARD
AND HAVE FUN. YOU DESERVE IT.

if not
now,
when?

THANK YOU TO ALL MY FRIENDS AND FAMILY THAT I MENTIONED EARLIER. YOU'VE LITERALLY BEEN HERE SINCE THE BEGINNING OF THIS JOURNEY.

THANK YOU TO MARIAN LIZZI. IT IS SUCH A DREAM WORKING WITH YOU!

Cristina Vanko is 27 years old and maybe an adult? She's the author of "Hand-lettering for Everyone" (very adult) and an ice-cream aficionado (ageless). She works in Chicago as an art director, illustrator, and letterer. Though she's still figuring out what it means to be an adult, she's pretty sure she'll reach adult status when she stops doing laundry at her parents' house.

@CRISTINAVANKO | CRISTINAVANKO.COM
@ADULTISHBOOK